SUCCESS SECRETS 7

for Every

WOMAN

in

LEADERSHIP

SIMPLE TACTICS FOR LEADERSHIP SUCCESS

BERNICE BOYDEN, SPHR, CEC

The Masterful Leader
Bernice@themasterfulleader.com
www.themasterfulleader.com

ISBN: 978-0-98269-910-2

LIMITS OF LIABILITY AND DISCLAIMER OF WARRANTY
The author and publisher shall not be liable for your misuse of this material. This book is strictly for informational and educational purposes.

WARNING – DISCLAIMER
The purpose of this book is to educate and entertain. The author and/or publisher do not guarantee that anyone following these techniques, suggestions, tips, ideas, or strategies will become successful. The author and/or publisher shall have neither liability nor responsibility to anyone with respect to any loss or damage caused, or alleged to be caused, directly or indirectly by the information contained in this book.

THANK YOU....

I dedicate this book to my loving family...

My mom and dad for always believing in me and telling me
that I could do whatever my heart desired;

My husband Alex and children, Alexis and Alex for being my
inspiration. Thank you for believing in my big dreams and
going on this journey with me! It's not over, hold on tight!

P.S. Also, a big thank you to Milana for all of her help,
guidance and support.

TABLE OF CONTENTS

PREFACE

WHY SHOULD YOU READ THIS BOOK?

Do you face professional challenges? Do you want to achieve a healthy work-life balance? Are you looking for advice and tips that can help you deal with office politics? Are you a woman to whom personal success is important?

If yes, then you have every reason to read this book!

In today's competitive dog-eat-dog world, everyone has to walk the line between achieving personal fulfillment and professional success. As a woman, your job becomes even more challenging as you have to fight gender prejudices, learn when to use soft power and when to get aggressive, and deal with office politics with confidence and tact.

Having been a part of the corporate world for many years, I realized that there was a need for women in leadership to find their own personal success within their job. I know that there are lots of books in the market telling women about how to be successful professionals_the business aspects, what to do and what not to do in order to achieve professional success_but there is very little material out there about personal success. I will show you how to fill this gap between the professional and the personal.

Most professional women that I have come across over the last decade like their profession but remain unhappy or unfilled because the work stress prevents them from enjoying a fulfilling personal life. Another problem I have often heard from professional women is that sometimes they feel stuck in their jobs and are not sure which way to go in order to grow in their careers.

Through this book I hope to show my fellow women professionals how to achieve both professional success and personal fulfillment. I do not mean to preach, nor do I pretend that I know every trick in the book that will help you reach the pinnacles of success. All that I intend to do through this book is to share whatever I have learned about survival and success in the professional world.

The strategies I have suggested in the book are practical and do-able_because they are all tried and tested by me. I have also shared several personal stories to illustrate my points and to help you understand how a little change in attitude can bring about major changes in your life.

I hope that by the time you finish reading this book you will have a better awareness of yourself and what keeps you ticking. The problem is that a lot of us start identifying ourselves solely with our professions, but the truth is that all of us are individuals in our own right and have a life and personality that goes beyond our professional description. The irony of the situation is that you can truly achieve professional success only if you feel whole and complete as an individual. You need to see yourself beyond the narrow confines of your professional role and responsibilities, because it's only when you let yourself grow personally that you will be able to achieve greater professional success. It is my sincere hope that my book helps you find the happiness and success you deserve.

Good luck and happy reading!

Bernice Boyden
The Leader's Confidante

CHAPTER I

THE SEVEN STRATEGIES OF SUCCESS

Success in any career is not dependent on monetary incentives and promotions alone, personal satisfaction also plays a huge role in determining how successful or unsuccessful you feel. Based on my personal experience I'd say that in order to build a successful career, you would need seven essential strategies. These strategies are nothing but basic techniques and approaches that you need to develop in order to ensure that you are able to reap and enjoy the monetary, personal and emotional benefits of success.

WHAT ARE THE SEVEN STRATEGIES?

I have learned a lot of lessons in my corporate career the hard way by practicing the standard method of trial and error. Through this book, however, I hope to pass on the knowledge that I have gathered through my experiences, so that you can learn from my mistakes instead of making your own and avoid the repercussions of those mistakes on your career.

The seven strategies I recommend here are a gist of all that I have learned in my career.

STRATEGY #1
CREATE BOUNDARIES AROUND YOUR SPACE, TIME AND RESPECT

You may have ten tasks to accomplish in one day, but you won't be able to accomplish much unless you prioritize them and block some time off for each one on your list. This is all the more important if you are in a job that requires you to interact with or counsel/advise a lot of people.

Let me give you an example to explain this. Let's say you work in the HR department of an organization. Now, not every aspect of your job would relate to dealing with people; there are reports to prepare, presentations to make, e-mails to respond to, and meetings to attend. You won't be able to accomplish any of these things efficiently and well within the stipulated deadline unless you create boundaries around yourself. This, in simple terms, means that you need to block off time during your office hours to focus on tasks that require your complete attention. The time boundaries you create will let people know that you are available, but not always on their schedule or at their convenience. You need to teach your clients/employees how to respect your boundaries, by your actions. I'll teach you some strategies on how to do this in chapter 2.

STRATEGY #2
Maintain a Healthy Work-Life Balance

All work and no play makes life tough! While working hard and fulfilling your ambitions are important, you won't experience much joy in your life if work is all that you do. It is extremely important, not just for the sake of your personal sanity but also for long-term success in your career. If your work life starts taking its toll on your personal life, it won't be too long before you reach the stage of burnout. Lack of ideas, lethargy, loss of enthusiasm . . . these are some of the most common symptoms of this stage, and none of them sound like ingredients that would go into any recipe for success!

STRATEGY #3
Manage Stress and Burn Out

Like it or not, stress is like a necessary evil. While just the right amount of it can push us to get things done, excessive stress does just the opposite. It's a well-known fact that people are unable to deliver their best when they are too anxious or nervous (side effects of stress); moreover, excessive stress also gives rise to several physical and mental ailments. What makes the problem worse is that we as women tend to take on a lot more stress than do our male counterparts, even more so if we are mothers. Therefore, you need to know how to manage your stress and avoid burnout so that you can not only achieve success but also enjoy its fruits.

STRATEGY#4
Stay Real

When working in any profession or organization you are bound to find yourself in situations where losing yourself in order to "gel" with the crowd may seem like the most tempting option available. The downside of this is that if you do it often enough you are likely to forget who you really are! So, why is it so important to stay real? I believe the most important reason is that unless you stay true to yourself you are likely to lose your credibility and integrity_two of the most important qualities for long-term success and personal fulfillment.

STRATEGY #5
Build Your Value

In any organization your perceived value is your real value! In order to grow in your career and increase your influence in your organization you need to brand yourself_play on your strengths, grab every opportunity that allows you to flaunt them without appearing pompous, take credit where you deserve it, and make sure that your boss knows just how hard you are working! After all, unless people know what you do and what you are good at, you will remain an invisible cog in the wheel.

STRATEGY #6
Navigate the Murky Waters of Office Politics

Though office politics is a dirty word_actually, two!_we unfortunately can't deny its existence. When you have a group of ambitious people working together, each with different personality traits and flaws, conflicts are bound to arise. Competition for the same prize, be it promotion or recognition, also creates conflict of interest, which is one of the root causes of office politics. Gender stereotypes only add to it.

For the sake of your professional growth and peace of mind, it is important for you to develop strategies to protect yourself from the nasty side effects of workplace politics.

STRATEGY #7
Now Your Players

You can't really hope to win a game unless you know what makes your players tick! Similarly, if you are in a managerial position you need to understand what makes your team members/clients tick and what puts them off, not just to make your job of dealing with them easier but also for your personal and professional growth. If you are aware of what kind of people your key players are (front-line employees to upper management), you will be able to build better relationships with them and leverage those relationships to increase your influence in the organization.

The points I have stated above may seem simple and straightforward, and there is no denying the fact that they truly are.

However, using these strategies to your advantage requires real skill and talent. For instance, all of us know that in order to really grow in our careers we need to put our foot down now and then_but how many of us know how to do it? We are all aware of the fact that unless there is balance between our personal and professional lives, we will not be able to truly enjoy the fruits of success. But then again, how many of us actually know how to achieve this balance? And more importantly, even if we know how to do it, how many among us actually manage to live fulfilling personal and professional lives?

In the subsequent chapters, therefore, I will be addressing each of the above-mentioned points in detail, so that I can share my "how-to" knowledge with you. Hopefully by the time you finish this book you will not only be aware of the raw materials that you need in order to build a successful career in the profession/business you are in, but will have gained the knowledge necessary to put them to the test.

CHAPTER 2

CREATE BOUNDARIES AROUND YOUR SPACE, TIME AND RESPECT

The key to creating your boundaries is to stay focused on your main goals for the day. This means you need to prioritize your tasks and focus on those that are the most important for you considering your present circumstances and workload.

For instance, imagine a scenario in which you have just come back to your office after a half-day meeting, only to realize that there are some 200+ mails waiting to be read in your inbox. Just as you settle down to sift through them and respond to the important ones, a team member pops in saying that he has one quick question. Now, his question may or may not be quick_ the discussion could take five minutes or forty-five minutes, depending on the situation your colleague wants to discuss. It's only by the time you are in the middle of the discussion that you will be able to figure out whether or not the said issue was urgent, but by then you would already have wasted the time you had blocked off for an "important" task.

If only you had shut your door to indicate that you were busy, and refrained from answering your phone calls for about an hour after coming back from your meeting, not only would you have been able to catch up on your work or finish an important task but would also have found it easier to listen to and sort out your team member's issues later on.

Having worked in different managerial positions over the many years, I realize how difficult it is to turn down someone who has come to you for help. But the fact is that unless you learn how to say "No" when necessary, you will find yourself fighting a constant battle with time_and, more often than not, you'll end up losing.

How to Create Boundaries?

Now that we have established that creating boundaries is important, the next vital question is, how do we create these boundaries? Here are some time-tested strategies.

Learn to Say No Without Being Offensive

The biggest problem most of us have with saying "No" is that we are fearful of offending the person who has sought us out. However, it is the way you put your foot down that makes all the difference in your interpersonal relationships.

Remember to be respectful when you are saying no; don't give your clients/colleagues the impression that you feel their request is frivolous or not important enough, and most importantly, make it clear that you consider their request/issue after you are done with the job at hand. And needless to say, before you decide to say "No" to someone you must prioritize your tasks.

For instance, let's say you are working on a hot and heavy matter in your department and a manager from another department comes to you with some urgent issue that she was with your department. You don't necessarily have to drop everything you are doing to look into her case. The best strategy in fact would be to hear her out and then tell her that you will sort out her issue as soon as you are done with what you are working on currently. It is of course important to use discretion at this point to figure out whether the "urgent matter" is actually urgent enough for you to put on the top of your priority list!

BALANCE YOUR ACCESSIBILITY

While it is a good thing to be easily accessible to your team members, being too accessible can be a bit of a problem. If you have people constantly walking in and out of your office space, you will find it difficult to get anything done. For instance, if you are trying compile a report and people keep popping in and out of your office or your phone keeps ringing, you'll find it very difficult to concentrate on the task at hand, and in all likelihood you will either miss your deadline or will end up burning the midnight oil!

My advice therefore is that when you need to get something done, block off some time_e.g., shut your door and don't answer the phone for that period of time. When your door is open, that's as good as a sign that says, "Hey, I'm available, come on in!"
It does feel odd initially when you start making yourself unavailable for a certain period of time every day, but the fact is that you are not taking this time off to meet any personal obligations_you are still doing official work. All of us have certain tasks, like preparing project reports, presentations, investigations, etc, that re-

quire our complete attention, and accomplishing those tasks is also an equally important part of our jobs.

In the long run, this strategy of blocking off time actually proves to be excellent for efficient time management and even helps in increasing your productivity and efficiency. In fact, by creating these divisions in your time and taking care of the necessary things that you have on your plate on a particular day you will be able to give more attention to the clients/team members who seek you out.

To quote a personal example here, I once had a habit of making sure that I answered every phone call and e-mail addressed to me. Now obviously a habit like this is not easy to keep up with. Funny as it sounds, during my work hours I actually used to look like an octopus, as I tried to do everything at once, reading and answering e-mails while trying to hold a phone conversation; worst of all, despite my hands and ears being busy, I would not turn down anyone who walked into my office, and would put one of my calls on hold to hear what they had to say! As you can well imagine, I felt harassed, exhausted, and frustrated. So I started following the strategy of balancing my accessibility. I would close the door for a certain period of time every day and allow my phone to go into voice mail as I answered my e-mail or worked on a report. Guess what? I got more work done in two hours than I did in eight hours previously. Try it!

TEACH YOUR TEAM MEMBERS/CLIENTS THE BOUNDARIES OF RESPECT WITH YOU

Respect, it is said, can't be demanded but is commanded. Though in most organizations employees/clients look up to their team leaders, occasionally you may come across individuals who may that they can get away with things just because you are soft-spoken or a woman.

For instance, you may find yourself stuck in a situation between two of your team members who are upset with each other and they may use you as the person to vent it all out on. While being a good listener is a required quality for any one in a managerial position, you may find that virtue being taken advantage of, especially in situations like this. I can say from experience that sometimes things can turn ugly when the people involved start getting really loud or angry and you find yourself being at the receiving end of it all.

Sometimes it is essential to draw clear lines and let people know that you will not tolerate being talked to in an inappropriate manner. Make it clear that you expect a certain level of respect and civility in your interactions with your fellow team members. Of course, you must also remember to treat everyone else the way you want to be treated_that in fact, is the best way to command the respect you deserve.

The same rule applies to interactions with clients and customers as well. While it is important to treat people who give you business with respect, it is also essential that they know what lines they can't cross with you. Give a firm and polite reminder whenever someone crosses the line of civility with you.

YOU CAN'T BE AT EVERYBODY'S BECK AND CALL

This essentially is an extension of the "Balance your Accessibility" principle. As good as we women are at multitasking, it is important to remember that you can't please everyone and there is a limit to how much you can do. If you try to answer every phone call and respond to everyone's request for your time, you will not be able to accomplish much.

Unless you make it clear to your clients/team members that, while you are willing to address their issues, you cannot be available at all times or at their convenience, they will not realize the importance of your time, nor will they learn to respect your schedule. It is of course important to send this message in a non-offensive way (i.e. posting your schedule or blocking time off on your Outlook calendar).

I've done this: balanced my accessibility by sticking to my schedule as best as I can and prioritizing my workload. So what you need to do is to make your own workable plan and follow it through.

These strategies may sound too simplistic, but they are vital for not only your survival at the work place but also your long-term career growth. Obviously, following them is easier said than done because you will need to be at your diplomatic best in order to make sure that you don't offend too many people when you start creating boundaries for yourself.

You may also wonder, What is the worst that can happen if I don't create professional boundaries? The answer is: a lot! For one, if you say "Yes" to everyone but are unable to meet your commitments, you will eventually be labeled lackadaisical and inefficient. Even if you try your hardest to meet all your commitments and work from sunrise to sunset, eventually your productivity will start going down because there is only so much stress that your body and mind can take.

So, the moral of the chapter is: Do your best at work but don't overwork yourself, as it won't do you or your organization any good.

CHAPTER 3

WORK LIFE BALANCE

W hen we start in our careers no matter what profession we choose, we all try to do our best to climb the ladder in the fastest possible manner. What often happens as a result is that we end up focusing too hard on our careers and forget that we have a life outside our work place as well. While burning ambition can sustain you for the initial few years, eventually you'll reach a stage where you will find yourself constantly battling with physical and mental fatigue.

I made the same mistake early in my career and I paid the price. My husband had to travel frequently for work, I had two young children and a grandmother to take care of at home, and at work I had a million people on my back for ten hours a day! All I remember of those years is that I worked constantly and that, by the time I got home, I was physically drained and emotionally unavailable to my loved ones yet I still had to push myself to take care of my responsibilities. I started falling sick frequently and my personal life, as you can well imagine, had little joy in it.

A lot of people have asked me if I give so much importance to work-life balance because I am a woman, and the answer I give is yes. For women striking a balance between their personal and professional lives is all the more important because we are "typically" the primary care givers at home too. However, this doesn't mean that achieving this balance is not important for single women. After all, what do we work for? Prosperity, happiness, satisfaction and/or independence, right? So, what really is the point of a job that doesn't even allow us the time to enjoy our prosperity? Or takes away the very life that we seek to make joyful?

Some people learn this lesson the hard way. I had a co-worker, married, with no children, who would just drown herself in work. She was the first to reach the office in the morning and the last to leave. Obviously this meant that she had very little time for her husband and probably hardly ever got any "me" time. Eventually, her work started taking its toll on her marriage and health. She started falling sick frequently and marital conflicts became a part of her daily life. It was only when she realized that her marriage was on the verge of a complete breakdown that she stated creating boundaries around herself.

I quoted this example here to explain how waiting until you are at the point of losing things you hold most dear to decide to get your personal life back in order is not the best way to achieve a healthy work-life balance! It is better to take remedial measures before your life starts spiraling out of control.

The vital question now is how do you create this Work-Life Balance? Based on my personal experience I'd suggest the following three strategies.

LEARN HOW TO MANAGE YOUR TIME

The keywords of time management are focus and clarity. This means that you must be clear about what is more important and when, and you must be focused enough to stick to the daily goals you have set for yourself.

So if you usually find yourself wishing that there were more than twenty-four hours in the day . . . then I can bet you are not managing your time well! The main reason why most of us fail to accomplish our goals or are unable to strike a balance between our personal and professional lives is because either we fail to prioritize our tasks or are unable to remove "time-drainers" from our schedule.

Time-drainers are typical activities that we waste time on. They can include excessively long conference calls, unproductive meetings, an obsessive e-mail checking habit, surfing the net, etc.

Once you have identified them, you need to come up with the best solution to handle them. Here's some advice that you might find useful:

- *Bow out.* If you find yourself stuck in long conference call and meeting where your input is not really required or where you have done your part but are still expected to hang around because the others are still talking, bowing out politely is a good idea. As long as you don't make a habit of it, getting out of a prolonged conference call once in a while should not reflect badly on you. The same rule applies to unproductive meetings as well.

- *Prioritize e-mails.* E-mails are in some ways a necessary evil: you need to check your inbox and make sure you don't miss important mail, but at the same time you also have to sift through the unimportant ones to read those that are urgent or contain important information. You can reduce the time-draining potential of e-mail either by speaking to your IT person and getting your inbox organized in such a way that the e-mails from specific people (for instance, your boss, senior managers, or others whose messages tend to require a prompt response) get delivered directly to a certain folder, or request your upper management to flag the mail that they send to you as "urgent," so that you can read the most relevant e-mail first and then look through the others as you have time.

- *Make a list.* The most tried and tested time management strategy of course is making 'to-do lists' or detailed daily plans. Needless, to say that you must discipline yourself to follow the plans you have drafted on paper. What I've found useful is to write everything down in my calendar, so that I can check things off as I complete them and I know exactly what I have to work on the next morning. This really helps me see my progress and keep track of where I need to focus.

- *Take a break.* Time management, however, does not mean that you have to try and cram in as much work as you can in your office hours. After all, to keep your mind active and alert you need to take little breaks from time to time. A good time management plan therefore must take these breaks into account.

- *Relax over lunch.* Recharging or re-balancing yourself

during your transit or lunchtime is also an effective time management strategy. For instance, you can listen to your favorite music or book while driving to work, catch up with a friend while you are stuck in a traffic jam or read a novel/book on a subject that interests you during your lunch break. I recharge by listening to music_this helps me to unwind. However, everyone is different, so try and figure out what relaxes you the most and fit in that activity in your transit or lunch time.

- *Visualize peace.* A colleague of mine used to practice visualization exercises, like imagining herself in a beautiful valley or a gorgeous garden. These exercises are almost like meditation, except that instead of focusing

- *Laugh.* Sometimes talking to a friend or a family member who makes you laugh can also help. After all, there is no better antidote for lethargy and stress than a good hearty laugh.

FOCUS ON HOW YOUR WORK-LIFE BALANCE CAN ACTUALLY ENERGIZE YOU

A big reason why the best-made time management plans fail is lack of planning. However, if you keep focusing on the end result, you will find it easier to follow these plans through. The purpose of a time management plan is to keep you healthy, happy, and energized, so that you can perform well professionally and enjoy a fulfilling personal life.

If you use up all your energy at work, you won't have much left to give to your loved ones and family, least of all to yourself.

Therefore you need to make sure that you conserve some energy at work and follow your time management plan so that you are not completely drained by the time you reach home.

I personally feel that focusing on things that you will have time for if you are able to strike a balance between your personal and professional life is an extremely effective motivation strategy. For instance, if you enjoy playing a sport, then focus on that to help you get through the day; or if at-home time is most important to you, think about spending quality time with your family and friends to keep your motivation levels from plummeting.

MAKE SURE THAT YOUR WORK DOESN'T START COMPETING WITH YOUR PERSONAL LIFE

How many times do you say "No" to family or social events because of your work? How often do you turn down dates or catch-up sessions with friends because you simply don't have the time? When was the last time you played a board game with your kids or helped them with homework? How often are you able to attend your children's school functions? If your work has been preventing you from doing simple things with your loved ones, then you are leading an extremely unbalanced life.

Apart from being there for your family, it is also extremely important to take out "me-time" in order to live a healthy and balanced life. Unfortunately, we as women generally end up compromising on our "me-time" in order to balance our personal and professional lives. That's where we make the biggest mistake in terms of work-life balance. The fact is that to achieve long-term success and gain personal fulfillment you must feel at peace with yourself, and that will be difficult unless you give time to yourself. It's not an act of selfishness, but of self-love!

This "me-time" could be for anything that you like doing: reading, playing a sport, or simply watching TV. If you are not getting even an hour in a day for yourself, then it's time you start setting your priorities right.

FIND YOURSELF - FIND WHAT MAKES YOU TICK

You are probably thinking, "It's all very well to say Get your priorities right! But how do I go about it? How do I decide what's important and what's not?" As much as I'd like to tell you exactly how to go about it, I am afraid I can't, because setting your priorities is a very subjective, personal matter.

You can find the answer by looking within and asking yourself, "What is it that makes me happy?" Make a list of everything that brings you joy. Then ask yourself this question: "Is my job allowing me to do those things?" More importantly, try to figure out how much happiness and satisfaction you get from your work. This little exercise will help you figure out exactly what you need to include in your schedule to ensure that you are able to live a healthy and balanced life.

To make this really work, you need to constantly remind yourself of what your priorities are. I would recommend that you make three copies of this "happiness list" and keep one in your planner, one someplace where you can see it every day at home, and one on your work-desk.

GET CREATIVE AND TALK TO YOUR MANAGER

Unfortunately, not all organizations value their employees' work-life balance. If the one you work in falls in this category, then you need to make the extra effort yourself. You are probably wondering how can you go about doing that without jeopardizing your job, right? My suggestion is that you should discuss your case with your manager and show him/her what the organization has to gain by enabling you to have a balanced life.

Every organization wants productive and efficient employees. You need to make your manager see that, if you follow the schedule you have made for yourself (which also allows time for your personal needs and commitments) you will be far more productive. The key is to talk in terms of increasing productivity_how your schedule will benefit the company, instead how it will benefit you.

Your productivity or efficiency depends not only on your motivation levels but also on your physical fitness and emotional satisfaction. Unless your life is balanced, you will not be able to give your best at work. You will treat most of your professional tasks as mere compliance issues and life will eventually become simply about going through the motions. Doesn't sound like a very happy state of existence, does it? However, when you explain these facts to your manager, you will have to talk backwards, as in discussing how you need to follow a schedule that allows you to create professional boundaries (discussed in the previous chapter) as well as time to take care of your physical and emotional health, in order to perform better. Needless to say, you will have to back your claims with tangible results.

A personal story to emphasize my point: I used to work in an organization where my manager did not believe in work-life balance. For my manager, work was her life; she put in 60+ hours of work a week_and she expected everyone our team to emulate her! Obviously, none of us wanted a life like that, so my co-workers and I put our heads together and came up with a strategy plan that showed how we could be more productive if we worked in reasonable time frames. We presented it to our manager, and guess what? It worked!

Of course, this strategy will only work for you if you approach your manager with other team members or if you individually are extremely valuable to your organization. This means that you need to create value for yourself; I will discuss how to go about this in chapter 6.

It is important to remember that your work is a part of your life, and not vice versa. So do your best at your job, but please don't let it overtake your life.

CHAPTER 4

How to Manage Stress and Avoid Burn Out

Like it or not stress is something all of us have to deal with in our professional lives. The pressure of deadlines and meeting targets, office politics, personal responsibilities all contribute to our stress levels.

How to Identify That You Are Stressed?

A lot of women I have come across are on the verge of complete burnout, but they don't even realize that they are stressed. The problem usually is that we get so used to the way of life we have adopted that we are unable to separate stress from our routine.

As I discussed in chapter 3, I was in this situation early in my career: working non-stop both at home and at my workplace, I got so lost in going through the motions that I did not even realize that I had almost burned out! I became very ill that when it hit me.

If you can identify with this situation, then what you need to do is to re-examine and re-evaluate your goals so that you get greater clarity about what you really want from life and how much is stress affecting your life. To start, ask yourself the following questions:

- How different are you today in terms of your goals, enthusiasm and ambitions from when you started your career?

- Have you reached the goal you hoped to?

- Has your enthusiasm level diminished to the point that all you care about is going through the motions and getting your pay check?

- Are you anywhere close to fulfilling your ambition?

- Do you feel mentally too tired or fatigued to come up with new ideas?

- How is your home life?

- Are you emotionally available to your family after you get back home?

- On a scale of 1 to 10, how would you rate your physical stamina and mental strength after an average workday?

If through your answers you discover that:

- There is a huge gap between what you were when you had just come aboard your professional boat and where you are now;

- Your productivity and efficiency levels are declining or have declined;

- The quality of your personal life is not satisfying;

then it means that stress is taking its toll on your life, and you know you have some work to do.

How to Deal with Stress?

There are several simple stress management strategies that I have come up with based on my personal experience and interaction with my work colleagues. The techniques suggested below are practical methods that I, and many of my co-workers, have used to avoid burnout.

Take a Relaxed Lunch

While it's essential to manage your office time effectively and eliminate time-drainers from your schedule, it is also equally important to give your mind and body a chance to relax a little from time to time. The office lunch hour provides an excellent opportunity to do the just that, so you should try to make the best of it. Leave your desk and join your colleagues in the office cafeteria, go out for lunch, talk a walk, or work out.

A lot of women get into the bad habit of having lunch at their desks and end up cramming "time-saving" activities like reading e-mail, making phone calls, grocery lists, or other such tasks. The problem is that in the long run these activities backfire! After all, there is a limit to the pressure that your mind and body can take. Forcing yourself to work without taking adequate breaks will eventually affect your mental alertness, physical fitness, and consequently your efficiency. In fact, I can say from experience that people who take time off for their lunch are actually able to accomplish more in the latter of half of the day than those who cram in work-related tasks or errands during their precious lunch hour.

TAKE ON AN ADDITIONAL PROJECT

All right, the idea may sound completely outrageous at the outset_but trust me, it works! You are probably thinking, How will taking up an extra project help me if I am already under so much work stress? The fact is that a lot of times stress is a by-product of monotony. Doing the same kind of tasks over and over again often leads to boredom, and that in turn has a direct and adverse effect on our motivation levels. A new challenge in these situations often proves to be just what the doctor ordered!

Let me illustrate this point with a practical example. Let's say you run your own consultant firm and have mostly fashion stores as your clients. You might consider diversifying your client portfolio to make things more challenging and interesting. Or perhaps you are the employee relations person in the organization: you interact with employees and try to smooth out interdepartmental and interteam issues day in and day out. It's obvious that such a job can become extremely stressful. Now suppose your department needs people for a new policy-making project. I'd suggest you volunteer for it, so that you can get to do something different, challenging, and productive.

Of course it would mean that you will have to re-work your schedule and make space for the new project, but in the long run, taking on new challenges will help increase your work satisfaction and consequently reduce your stress levels

ORGANIZE YOUR OFFICE AND WORK SPACE

Clutter emanates negative energy and stress. If your office space is cluttered with files and papers (even if you know what is lying where) you will end up feeling overwhelmed with work and stress. After all, not only is a messy office space hard on the eyes, it is also extremely difficult to find anything amidst clutter (this inevitably leads to waste of precious time and, consequently, stress). A clean and clutter-free workspace will also help you stay more focused on the tasks at hand.

PRACTICE TIME MANAGEMENT TECHNIQUES

You won't find yourself constantly fighting a losing battle against time if you learn and start practicing effective time management techniques that I have suggested in chapter 3.

FIGURE OUT IF YOU ARE INTERNALIZING YOUR JOB

I have seen this happen with a lot of my women colleagues. In all businesses, sometimes we have to make decisions that affect other people's careers and even livelihoods. It's not surprising, then, that a lot of women end up taking on too much pressure and /or find themselves getting emotionally involved with situations that they have to deal with.

While empathy is a good thing, sometimes we as women overdo it! I know, because I used to do it too_in fact, even today there are times when I carry the mental pressures of my work home with me. We are all humans, and empathy comes naturally to most of us, so it is natural to feel bad about making tough decisions. Having been through it myself, I also understand how difficult it is to leave your office stress behind at times when the work pressure is intense. But the fact is that you need to make a conscious effort to keep your emotions in check while making business decisions if you want to survive and grow in your career.

I would suggest that you spend a few minutes of quiet time, or take up de-stressing activities like yoga or meditation, to deal with the pressures of your job. Find whatever works best for you.

The key to dealing with stress is catching it before it starts getting unmanageable. Burnout, after all, is a result of months or years of untreated stress and anxiety. Figuring out the signs early on and taking steps to reduce your stress levels is therefore the best way to avoid burnout. Everyone reaches their burnout point at different levels, so this is something that you must keep an eye on.

CHAPTER 5

STAYING REAL

What happens when, in an effort to please everyone, you become someone that even you don't recognize? Everyone wants you on their side, wants you to agree with what they believe in and ultimately tuck you in their little pocket. If you don't stand your ground and remain in that neutral space, you will be sucked in and will become someone else...someone you don't even like!

We play several roles at work and in our personal life: mothers/spouses, negotiators with our bosses and clients, counselors and guides for our team members, communicators, administrators, etc.

Amidst playing all these roles on a daily basis, maintaining a sense of self may become difficult. However, unless you stay true to yourself, not only will you end up losing your sense of focus and self-confidence, but will also hamper your career growth in the long run. After all, how long can you go on acting a part and suppressing your real self? Eventually you will either slip up or get tired.

How to Stay Real

In all honesty there is no magic formula that can help you stay true to yourself; all I can give you are a few tried and tested suggestions.

Love Yourself for Who You Are

Self-confidence is essential in order to stay true to yourself. After all, only if you are comfortable in your skin and are happy with who you are will you be able to stand your ground in the trickiest of situations. I know from personal experience that often there are occasions in which it would be a lot easier to lose yourself and be one of the crowd. Your self-confidence is what will save you from losing yourself in such situations.

Ask Yourself "Have I Sold My Soul to the Devil?"

I don't mean to sound offensive, but it is a fact that sometimes to climb up the ladder we try to project an image that isn't really us, either by acting like one of "the crowd" to gain acceptance or by molding our behavior according to the expectations of the people we wish to please. The problem is that the charade often doesn't last long_people eventually see through it and the consequence is obviously loss of trust!

The fact is that even though straightforward people may take a little longer to climb the first few steps of the ladder, they command greater respect. In fact, if you are true to yourself and your beliefs you will find that people confide in you more, and eventually success will come. Perhaps your progress will be a little slow, but what's important is that it will not be at the cost of your dignity and happiness.

So I suggest you ask yourself from time to time, "Is this really me? Am I acting this way only to appease certain people? Am I happy with the person I am becoming? Am I being true to myself?" There is nothing like objective introspection to keep you grounded and honest to yourself.

I have come across several people who have learned this lesson the hard way. One of my co-workers happened to be one such person. She was a "people pleaser." This lady wanted to be in everyone's good books, and constantly tried to please everyone by saying exactly what they wanted to hear. She was extremely ambitious and was eyeing an upper management position. Now, she felt the only way to achieve her goal was to be a "yes" person. This strategy of hers, however, led her into some extremely sticky spots: she tried to play on both sides and ended up playing people against each other. Eventually, her "yes sir/ma'am" strategy backfired and she was terminated for compromising a huge investigation.

Stay Neutral

You must be thinking that it's pretty easy to say "stay neutral," but the reality is that staying neutral and calm when your actions affect the lives of your colleagues is not really easy. Agreed_but if you want to survive and grow, it is essential that you keep your emotions and business separate.

In any business you may find yourself in situations when you have to make difficult decisions that may adversely affect your colleagues or someone you have become friends with. Getting emotional in such situations will not do you any good. I am in no way saying "don't have a heart," but you must have control of your emotions.

Unfortunately, staying neutral is a not a technique or skill taught in business schools; it is something that you need to develop yourself. From my personal experience, if you learn to separate sympathy from empathy, you will find it easier to stay neutral.

One strategy that I have developed (and it has worked well for me so far) is to focus on people's actions, and not on your personal equation with them or their personalities. Perhaps this example will make my point clearer. Suppose a person came to you with a problem. You sorted it out and in the process developed a personal liking for him. However, because of your organization's cost-cutting initiative, you have to terminate his employment. Now, implementing this decision will be tough, but if you focus on the actions of the person (less-than-adequate performance, of lesser value to the organization) rather than the person himself, you will find it easier to deal with the situation. Of course, it sounds like a cold-hearted thing to do, but you have to take such situations in stride because it's a part of your job. You cannot confuse empathy with sympathy.

An obvious question stems from this discussion: Should you become friendly with your colleagues and/or team members? Well, unless you want to live like a gladiator, being friendless in the work place is not a good idea!

So my suggestion is to try to stay neutral. You might find the following ground rules about office camaraderie useful:

- Do not share confidential business information with people you have befriended. Not only will getting too close to someone in the office affect your objectivity, but sharing such information can also land you in trouble.

- Be careful about who you let into your inner circle.
  You may be friendly with someone or have lunch with
  them on and off, and the person may take advantage of
  being seen with you to spread malicious rumors in the
  office or play politics using your name to benefit him or
  herself.

- Don't fall into the trap of playing favorites or even
  seeming to play favorites

CREATE YOUR PERSONAL SELF ETHICS LIST

This may sound like a very idealistic or bookish thing to do, but
I can tell you from personal experience that it works. All of us
need to make some compromises on the professional front, and a
little flexibility is essential for personal and professional success.
If you want to stay real and grounded, you need to know where
to draw the line. Create a list of the things that will never be an
option for you, for instance, "I won't set someone up to be terminated"; "I will not be fake"; "I will not spread malicious gossip"
and make sure that you stick by your list.

I admit that staying real or true to yourself requires a lot
of effort, so you may be wondering why you should invest so
much in sticking to your ethics despite the odds. Why not take
the easier way out, and change who you are according to your
circumstances? In all honesty, the most important reason is that
unless you are comfortable in your skin and let your real self
shine through, you will not be able to attain mental peace.

Another reason is that you can't hope to achieve much in any
career unless you stay true to yourself. Credibility and integrity

are among the most desired traits in any profession. After all, in order to take any business arrangement or professional relationship forward you must inspire trust in the people you interact with. Unless you appear genuine, no one is going to trust you!

If you are constantly projecting an image that isn't really you, sooner or later people will see through you, and trust would be the first casualty. After all, no one can trust a person who is not even honest to himself/herself!

The last, but definitely not the least, important reason why you should stay true to yourself is so that you can look into the mirror with pride. You will be able to respect yourself for your integrity, and will come across as a far more confident person. It's a well-known fact that women who appear confident and self-respecting command respect from others as well.

CHAPTER 6

BUILDING YOUR VALUE

Professional success and increased clout or influence in an organization go hand in hand. The more influential and powerful you become, the more successful you will be, and with greater success comes greater power and influence! So, if you want to increase your influence in the organization you work in, it is important to build your value.

This means that you must play to your strengths. When I started my career, I didn't know what my unique gift(s) were; it took me some years to find out that I was great at relationships and relationship building, which led me to get into employee relations. I also believe that we should constantly strive to develop ourselves, as that is the only way to grow and move forward in life. Your organization will value you if you build and create your own value.

So, to cut a long story short, the following are some of the best and most effective time-tested strategies that can help you build your value:

- Play to your strengths: If you don't know what they are, take some assessments to find out. (i.e. DiSC, HBDI, and MyersBriggs, StrengthsFinder)

- Create your own "brand value": Decide how you will be viewed in your organization.

- Convey yourself: (without brown nosing)

- Develop Yourself: If you don't, no one else will.

- Learn the business: Make the effort to learn how things tick.

PLAY TO YOUR STRENGTHS

It goes without saying that to play your strengths, you first need to know what you are good at! For most of us, discovering what we excel at takes time, experience, and introspection. While I can't help you gain experience, I can definitely tell you how to introspect so that you figure out what your assets or special gifts are.

In order to find out what you are good at, ask yourself the following questions:

What do I like? Most of us tend to be good at things that we like doing. The reason, obviously, is that when we enjoy doing something, motivation is never a problem and hard work doesn't require a lot of effort.

What are the things I have been good at? Look back at your life and make a note of things for which you were appreciated, whether or not they are directly connected with your present job. You never know which skill may come in handy.

Once you have made a list of things that you enjoy doing and are good at, see how you can use them in your job. For instance, if you are good at writing, you can volunteer for writing newsletters; if you feel you've got good people skills or have often played the role of confidant to your friends and family, employee relations may be the job where you'll find your niche.

Not only will playing to your strengths make you more valuable to the organization, you will also feel happier and more satisfied with your job.

BRAND YOURSELF

This really is an extension of the "play to your strengths" strategy. Just like you brand a product by creating value around its USP, you need to create your value by flaunting your USP. Your USP is your unique selling proposition, your uniqueness and what differentiates you from the pack. Take every opportunity that allows you to demonstrate your unique skills. For instance, if you are a good speaker or communicator, volunteer to undertake training assignments or play the commentator's part at your office sports event; work with people from other departments on projects where you know you can use your skills_grab every opportunity you can to show off your skills.

Admittedly, branding yourself does require extra effort, but trust me: the effort is worth it! The more you participate in projects or events that allow you to use your USP, the more people will become aware of it, and that is what branding is essentially about. People will associate you with your unique gift(s) and abilities, and every time a project comes up that requires the specialization you are known for, yours will probably be the first name that is recommended.

CONVEY YOUR WORTH

Most of us grow up believing that modesty is a virtue. While the statement is mostly true, being too modest also has its downside. To succeed in the competitive corporate world, you need to make sure that everybody knows what a good job you are doing. I do not mean that you should start acting pompous, because no one really appreciates that attitude. But you must make sure that your boss knows just how hard you are working.

Obviously, walking the fine line between conveying your worth and brown-nosing is not easy. However, from my experience it is possible if you follow the strategies listed below:

- *Be a reporter.* Create a weekly report that tells your boss what you have accomplished that week.

- *Keep score.* A lot of companies have a scorecard on which employees have to state what they have been doing during a specific time period_an official version of the report I mentioned above. This scorecard form offers an excellent opportunity to let your boss know what you have been doing, so make the most of it.

- *Share the news.* If you have been really successful with something, slip your achievement into in a casual conversation. For instance, if you were able to decrease turnover, creating a cost savings for the company, then let your management know that!

- *Blow your horn (quietly!)* Discuss your achievements in your feedback review meetings, but be sure to do it without sounding conceited or boastful. For example, tell your boss how you did something well and how you'd love to get an opportunity to use what you learned while accomplishing the said task.

- *As always... brand yourself.* If you run your own business, make sure you brand yourself and/or your business in a way that it reflects your USP; and your pamphlets, company literature, and website should be designed in a way that conveys your achievements, strengths, and USP.

Perception to most people is the only reality, so be sure you create the true perception that you are truly are an asset to your organization.

DEVELOP YOURSELF

In order to grow and prosper in your career you need to constantly work at developing yourself. This means learning new skills and even taking new courses if you feel the need.

Learning, whether it is through attending workshops, taking certification courses, job shadowing, or enrolling for a formal degree program, is essential for your career growth. You need to upgrade your skills and expand your knowledge constantly so that you can continue to progress.

Developing yourself can also help you overcome stagnation and the stress associated with it. So in effect, you are killing two_ or may I say three_birds with one arrow: improving your career prospects, beating stress and burnout, and enjoying greater work satisfaction.

LEARNING THE BUSINESS

No matter which department you work in, it is absolutely essential that you know and understand the business you are in. Without this knowledge it will be difficult for you to grow and reach a next level or senior level position.

Knowing your business is even more important if you work in a male-dominated organization, since you are likely to face situations where you will have to prove your knowledge of the business in order to be taken seriously.

Your knowledge about the business will also come in handy when you have to attend meetings with the leaders of the company. Not only will you be able to completely understand what they are talking about, but you will also be able to give valuable suggestions. For instance, when I worked in a call center environment and I took the time to understand the job; thus I was able to understand the need for policies around call time management and how it impacted customers. So whenever we had important management meetings I was able to give valuable and feasible suggestions backed by my understanding of how the business worked.

Now that we have established that learning the business you are in is important, the next most obvious question is, how should you go about doing it? Apart from the suggestions I have mentioned above (shadowing in departments and taking courses and certifications), you may try the following:

- *Read.* Read books and journals about the business/industry you are in.

- *Learn.* Follow business news and stay on top of the trends in the industry that your organization belongs to. In fact, keeping track of the developments in your industry can also help you build a greater rapport with your boss.

- *Share.* Consider forwarding interesting articles that talk about the impact of new developments in your industry to your boss. It will help in sending across the message that you understand the business and are genuinely interested in staying on top of things.

Your value in your organization depends on your attitude and approach to work. You can become an invaluable asset to your organization by following the right strategies; or you can remain a diligent but invisible worker: the choice is yours!

If you run your own business, then you already know how your organization works. However, it is important that you keep yourself updated on the latest industry trends. I would also advise you to make an effort to stay in the loop when it comes to dynamics between different individuals working for you (if it's a small business) or different departments (if it's a large organization).

CHAPTER 7

Navigating Through Office Politics

Like it or not, office politics are part of all companies/offices and navigating these murky waters is a learned skill.

What makes handling office politics an especially tricky business for women in managerial positions is that they need to walk the tightrope between keeping their team together and getting too involved in people's personal issues. They need to be aware of all the rumors and relationship issues in the office without being perceived as too associated with the people who are known gossipers and rumormongers. Throw some gender stereotypes into the mix, and office politics becomes even murkier!

How to Handle Office Politics

Having seen enough office politics in the time I have spent in the corporate world, I can suggest a few strategies that have worked for me and my colleagues.

ESCAPE THE WATER COOLER GOSSIP

As important as it is for you to be aware of what is happening in your office, it is equally important to remove yourself from places where gossip exchange takes place. At the very least, you shouldn't be seen hanging around people who are known to gossip. For example, if you are seen standing with a bunch of people maligning someone for his poor performance, your name will in all likelihood crop up later when the issue is being discussed (whether or not you spoke a word), especially if you are at a senior position. Needless to say, staying away from gossip is not an easy task_after all, being social people, we all feel drawn to such discussions. Perhaps what's even more difficult is keeping your mouth shut when you have a strong opinion about what is being said.

If you run your own business, then your participation or mere presence in malicious discussions can be extremely detrimental for your general employee morale. However, as I said previously, being aware of the employee dynamics is also crucial. So, the important question now is, how do you keep yourself aware without being seen around places where people tend to gossip? The answer is simple: Keep your eyes and ears open, spend some time on the work floor of various departments, observe people's behavior silently, and you will know all that you need to about office politics.

HANDLING OFFICE CONFLICTS DIPLOMATICALLY

Diplomacy (or neutrality) is a skill that every woman in a managerial position must possess. As a leader, you may find yourself stuck in a conflict between two employees/team members. Both may confide in you about their problems with the other and expect you to take their side; in fact, you may even find yourself agreeing with one person more than the other. However, being the person in a position of power, it is essential for you to stay neutral and be fair to all parties concerned; otherwise, before you realize it you will find yourself deeply involved in the conflict you were trying to solve. What's more, you will also have to make an extra effort to maintain your relationship with both the people concerned, because at some point they may start feeling that you aren't giving them enough attention or are taking the other person's side.

Diplomacy is a skill that will come in handy in this situation, because not only would you need to stay neutral while sorting the conflict out, you would also need to keep your eyes trained on the end result: that is, ensuring that the conflict does not affect anyone's productivity and efficiency, and that it gets resolved.

PROTECT YOUR REPUTATION

Whether you are in a managerial position or run your own business, in order to command respect from your employees/clients and teammates you must have impeccable integrity and credibility.

The vital question now is, how do you go about protecting your reputation? I'd suggest you live up to your standards, make sure that your behavior in the work place is beyond reproach, avoid becoming a part of office gossip or needless mud-slinging, be careful about who you befriend, be polite, and treat everyone around you with respect.

I have built my reputation by maintaining my fairness and consistency, and so far these qualities have worked for me. I have always believed that if I don't have anything else to offer, as long as I remain consistent and fair, I've maintained my credibility with my people.

CONFLICT MANAGEMENT (WHEN YOU ARE AT THE CENTER OF AN OFFICE CONFLICT)

There may be times when you find yourself at the center of a conflict, or the person at whom office gossip is directed. In such situations, you need to take a very cautious and sensible approach to protect your reputation and make sure that you are not accused of taking advantage of your position.

For instance, if you find yourself stuck in the middle of a conflict between two team-members and/or employees and one or both of them disagree with the advice you are offering and start an argument with you, take a step back and say, "Hey! We are adults here; let's sort it out calmly." If you notice that someone has raised their volume or are using an offensive tone, let them know in a calm but firm manner that you do not appreciate it and would rather talk once they have cooled down. The key is not to lose your temper and to stay calm when you find yourself at the center of a conflict.

Sometimes your advice may backfire, despite your best intentions. For instance, your suggestion about improving productivity in a particular department may not go down well with some of the employees. They may feel that you have betrayed their trust, and accuse you of being partial or unfair. So, what you need to do is to talk it out before the employees start a virtual gossip campaign against you. Personally, I believe in handling such situations by being straightforward and discussing facts. Confront the people who believe that you have been unfair to them, talk calmly, lay down the facts, and let them know that you have nothing personal against them and that the changes needed to occur.

The key is to avoid venting and look for solutions. What happens in most office conflicts is that people are under so much stress and pressure that they start off with venting and get carried away with that. Often comments and statements made during an emotional rant lead to more conflicts. The best way to deal with office conflicts that you find yourself personally involved in is to discuss solutions instead of going on and on about the problem.

REBUILD DAMAGED RELATIONSHIPS

Office politics become more complex when people start acting on the basis of their assumptions without making any effort to resolve the conflict. In my experience, when two employees have an issue with each other the best way to sort it out is by encouraging them to have a "positive confrontation."

The term "positive confrontation" may come across as an oxymoron because most of us see confrontation as something negative; we associate it with anger, arguments, and hurt feelings. The fact, however, is that a confrontation becomes what we make it. If you can discuss and sort out your issues calmly, then confrontation is the best way to resolve a conflict.

I, for one, have always been a believer in positive confrontations. After all, you can't survive in any job unless you are able to confront people without losing your temper. In an office environment, colleagues don't have to love each other or hold hands and sing together, but they do need to have mutual respect and tolerance for each other so that the efficiency of their team is not affected. For example, if a manager and employee have an argument about his/her performance, I would suggest that you encourage them to iron out their issues while you act as the mediator. It is important to impress upon employees that they need to act as mature professionals and not allow their personal issues to affect their performance and that of their team.

The next important question is, how do you repair a damaged relationship that relates to you? As I have said previously, the only way is to talk it out. Set up a time to meet the person who is upset with you, listen to his/her problems with an open mind, and put your case forward as honestly as you can. The key here is to reach a middle ground, a place from where both of you can leave the past behind and move on to new ventures.

For instance, whenever I have found myself in a situation that has become heated and where one party is unhappy with an action that I had to take, I have always approached the "offended" employee(s) to sort out the issue. I strongly believe in laying down all reasonable facts to avoid the possibility of a misunderstanding. Of course, people have not always been able to understand or see things from my point of view, but talking to them has always helped me sort out conflicts; worst-case scenario, we agree to disagree and move on from there.

It is important to remember that office relationships are just that: office relationships. They are about getting the work done. It will do you a lot of good if you don't get too emotionally involved and take things personally.

DO NOT LET GENDER STEREOTYPES AND POLITICS AFFECT YOUR CONFIDENCE

Like it or not, being a woman you may have to battle gender stereotypes at different times in your career. From personal experience, I feel it's best to develop a thick skin and not let people's prejudices affect your confidence. In case you feel gender politics is affecting your work efficiency, I would suggest positive confrontation as a solution.

MANAGE CONFLICTS, DON'T LET THEM MANAGE YOU!

Some of the most important questions that you need to ask yourself in this area are: Do you manage conflicts or do you let conflicts manage you? How do you react in conflict situations? Do you manage the conflicts that arise between you and your colleagues? Do you go in and act as the aggressor in helping to manage those conflicts, or do you just let those conflicts go and manage you? Do you confront or do you avoid?

To build a successful career in any profession you need to be able to confront people (positively though) so that you can resolve a conflict before it gets out of hand. Avoiding problems or hoping that they will sort themselves out on their own leads to bigger and more complex issues and the conflict eventually becomes so big that it starts controlling and managing you.

Of course to be able to manage conflicts successfully, you also need to stay in neutral territory. Taking sides, openly or covertly won't do you or your reputation any good. (For more information on how to stay neutral go back to chapter 5.)

CHAPTER 8

KNOWING YOUR PLAYERS

Knowing your players (team members and clients) is essential for your growth in any business/profession. You can't handle everyone with the same gloves. You must study each relationship and learn how to handle each effectively; after all, an approach that works for John won't necessarily work for Sally!

Just like in a game, you need to know what makes your players tick so that you can work as a team and bring the trophy home. In organizations, too, you need to understand what makes the employees tick; what gets them going and what puts them off. Knowing these things will help you more effectively deal with tricky conflict situations in your team and have better productivity. For instance, if you have a team member who is very outgoing, competitive, and ruthless, you have to be careful about how you give him feedback or approach him to sort out a situation. You will probably have to word your argument in a way that makes him realize that listening to your advice would help him perform better. On the other hand, if you have an employee who is timid and is unable to stand up for himself/herself, you'll need a different approach, different gloves.

In the long run, a sound knowledge of the strengths and weaknesses of your employees will also help you become more influential in your organization. Knowledge, after all, is power.

Case in point: I had a client manager who took everything personally; she got offended whenever someone approached her about an issue concerning her work or department. So when I had issues that I needed to handle with her, I always started our conversation by telling her that it was nothing personal, just a professional situation that we needed to deal with together. This helped me build a rapport with her, and she listened to me when I gave her advice on watching her professional behavior and being mindful of not taking everything personally.

Thus, knowing your players not only can help you figure out how to handle positive confrontations, develop professional relationships with different people, and build on your resources, but is also useful for increasing your brand value.

When you know what motivates people and what gets them going, it is easier to get them to be more productive for the organization and/or respond to your proposals the way you want. Understanding your employees' or clients' strengths will also help you make a positive contribution towards suggesting who should be chosen to take on new responsibilities and roles. Moreover, when you manage to resolve conflicts quickly or interact with someone in a way that makes them see your point of view, you will come across as someone who is persuasive and dynamic. Both qualities are essential for your growth in any career.

Another advantage of knowing your players is that it will help you decide whom you should align yourself with and who would be a good mentor for your personal growth.

GETTING TO KNOW YOUR PLAYERS

Now that we have made it amply clear that knowing your players is important, the next big question is, how do you go about it?

UNDERSTAND HOW THE BUSINESS AND THE EMPLOYEES WORK

Everyone has both good qualities and flaws; you will only be able to figure out what qualities in your clients/employees can make them valuable for your organization if you understand your business well. You have to know:

- who are the people you deal with;
- what are the goals and objectives of your organization;
- what strategies does your organization use to meet these goals; and
- how the personalities of people who work in the organization match up to these objectives.

Admittedly, this will take time and great observation on your part. And of course, in large organizations you can't keep track of every employee in every department; however, you can make an effort to get to know your key players.

LEARN YOUR PLAYERS LIKE A BOARD GAME

Learning your players like board game is a simple analogy for saying that you need to understand how each player affects the other. You need to be aware of their relationship and team dynamics. It's almost like a game of chess, where you need to have the foresight and vision to understand how one move will affect the rest of the game. For instance, you need to be able to pre-empt how a client/customer will react if you tell her that one of their employees is jeopardizing your business relationship with her, especially if the client/customer is fond of the person you are complaining against. If you are prepared for the reaction in such situations, you will be able to handle them better.

GET OUT AND MEET YOUR TEAM MEMBERS

In any managerial position, you need to make conscious efforts to get to know your team members. Waiting for a phone call or e-mail or for employees to always come to you with problems will not work well for you in the long run, as you will come across as disinterested and passive. Mingling with your team members at office functions and taking out time to sit on the floor to observe how they are working are better ways to get to know your players. Your genuine efforts to get to know your employees will also do wonders for your reputation, as you will come across as someone who is sincere and compassionate.

There are lots of simple ways through which you can get to know your players better. One practical strategy I have found useful is mingling with employees during company events or meetings. You may discuss family life (but keep it general and not too personal), sports, common hobbies, etc. Basically, the idea is to get people comfortable with you and send the message that you are like them, a normal person with a life outside the office.

Finally, try having an off-site meeting or team-builder, it will work wonders for your leadership.

GET TO KNOW YOUR CLIENTS/CUSTOMERS (FOR THOSE WHO RUN THEIR OWN BUSINESS)

Message boards on your website or building a Facebook profile are great ways to know and understand your clients. Keeping a guest book and participating in trade shows and local events are other ways through which you can build a rapport with your clients/customers.

Going to social events and networking with potential clients is also a good idea.

USE YOUR KNOWLEDGE

So, we have come to the conclusion that it is important to know your players, and we've even discussed how one can go about it, but one big question that still remains unanswered is, how do you use this knowledge to your advantage? Here's what I'd suggest:

PUT A POSITIVE SPIN TO EVERY CONVERSATION AND GET YOUR WORK DONE

People do not like being talked down to or threatened. Once you know what makes a person tick or what gets them going, you can put a positive spin in your conversation by presenting your facts in a way that appeals to them.

I'd like to share a personal story here that will help illustrate this point better. I once had a situation in which a group of managers was completely unhappy with their manager. They had some major issues but found it difficult to approach her; they didn't want to take their problems to her boss because they were afraid that the whole thing may backfire. One of them confided in me about it. I took the initiative to talk to the other managers so that I could understand exactly what their problems were.

After I had gathered all my facts, I went back to the group's manager. Now, I knew that she was a very emotional person and that if I told her that her managers had come to me with complaints about her, the whole confrontation would turn ugly and in all likelihood would backfire on the managers. So I began talking to her casually about success and how it is important to keep people in your team happy if you really want to achieve your goals. I kept my tone calm and understanding to get the point across to her, and it worked. Had I gone on the offensive and spoken to her in a threatening manner, not only would I have damaged my relationship with her, but I would have lost the trust of the managers who approached me as well. Needless to say, I would have completely failed at my job_all because I did not know my players well!

INCREASE YOUR INFLUENCE IN THE ORGANIZATION

Every professional woman wants to reach a position where she is heard and is a part of the decision-making process. In short, all of us want to be influential in our organization, so that we are not just rule-enforcers but partners in the growth and expansion of the organization. You can use your knowledge of people's personalities and professional qualities to become more powerful in the organization.

For instance, if you know that your boss is a rigid person who believes in following the tried and tested path, the best way to be heard in your organization would be to package your new ideas in such a way that they sound like minor deviations from what has been done successfully in the past. Adding research findings to your "deviation" will help you present your case even more successfully.

BRIDGE RELATIONSHIPS WITH YOUR CLIENTS/CUSTOMERS

Use your knowledge to build positive and effective relationships with your customers/clients. Knowing what to say to get another person interested or to persuade them to follow your advice will do wonders for your reputation.

Success comes to those who go out and seek it, so you have to take the right steps and use the most effective techniques or strategies to create a professionally satisfying and personally ful-filling life for yourself. Go get it!

CHAPTER 9

CONCLUSION

Success is all about the right attitude and mindset. I believe all of us have an untapped personal power that can help us achieve our goals and fulfill our ambitions, all we need are the right strategies to unleash the power.

The tips and suggestions I have shared in this book have helped me and numerous other women climb up the success ladder without making too many compromises with our personal lives.

Of course I wasn't born with the knowledge I have shared; neither did I learn everything I have talked about in a business school_experience has been my biggest teacher. This book has essentially been a compilation of all the lessons I learned from my experiences in the corporate world. It is my hope that you walked away with some real-life techniques and examples of how to have personal success!

Much Success,

Bernice

Bernice Boyden SPHR, CEC

Leadership Development Expert, Bernice Boyden, is fiercely committed to showing women in leadership on how to unleash their influence, gain more respect, confidence and be the "go-to" leader in the workplace. When you apply her "IT" Factor techniques, you will gain fast results at work and in your personal life. Guiding you to achieve the ultimate success as a leader with time tested, proven, and easy to learn tips—without you losing your sanity—is her passion and commitment. Bernice offers her no-nonsense, truth-telling, personal transparency and open communication style with all of her clients. Using her "best-friend" charisma, clients often feel like they've known Bernice all of their lives. For almost two decades while working as a Human Resources professional in several large Fortune 50 companies, Bernice had coached many elite-level leaders, implementing one-of-a-kind techniques that unleash strengths, maximize influence, increase respect and produce immediate results. Bernice is the author of two books, *Inspirations to Leadership-Words of Wisdom for the Leader in You* and *Seven Success Secrets for Every Woman in Leadership*.

Visit Bernice at www.themasterfulleader.com.